LIFE ON THE EDGE

# SLED DOG RACING

DANIELLE HAYNES

PowerKiDS press

Published in 2024 by The Rosen Publishing Group, Inc.
2544 Clinton Street, Buffalo, NY 14224



Portions of this work were originally authored by Kristen Nelson and published as *Racing the Iditarod.* All new material in this edition was authored by Danielle Haynes.

Editor: Danielle Haynes
Book Design: Rachel Rising

Photo Credits: Cover, Dmitry Kalinovsky/Shutterstock.com; Cover, pp. 1-32 David Arts/Shutterstock.com; Cover, pp. 1, 30-32 passion artist/Shutterstock.com; p. 4 Allen.G/Shutterstock.com; pp. 5, 7, 9, 11, 12, 15, 17, 19, 21, 23, 25, 27, 29 Olga_C/Shutterstock.com; p. 5 Nadezda Murmakova/Shutterstock.com; p. 7 REUTERS/Alamy Stock Photo; p. 8 Kid Dog Travel/Shutterstock.com; p. 9 https://commons.wikimedia.org/wiki/File:Alaska_iditarod_route.png; p. 10 prochasson frederic/Shutterstock.com; p. 11 lightman_pic/Shutterstock.com; p. 12 Maya2016/Shutterstock.com; p. 13 Germanova Antonina/Shutterstock.com; p. 13 hramovnick/Shutterstock.com; p. 15 Roger Asbury/Shutterstock.com; p. 17 Troutnut/Shutterstock.com; p. 19 ZUMA Press, Inc./Alamy Stock Photo; p. 20 Steve Jordan/Shutterstock.com; p. 21 Abaca Press/Alamy Stock Photo; p. 23 WorldFoto/Alamy Stock Photo; p. 25 Mikhail Pankov/Shutterstock.com; p. 27 REUTERS/Alamy Stock Photo; p. 29 Roman Babakin/Shutterstock.com.

Cataloging-in-Publication Data

Names: Haynes, Danielle.
Title: Sled dog racing / Danielle Haynes.
Description: New York : Powerkids Press, 2024. | Series: Life on the edge | Includes glossary and index.
Identifiers: ISBN 9781642827231 (pbk.) | ISBN 9781642827248 (library bound) | ISBN 9781642827255 (ebook)
Subjects: LCSH: Iditarod (Race)--Juvenile literature. | Sled dogs--Juvenile literature. | Sled dog racing--Juvenile literature.
Classification: LCC SF428.7 H394 2024 | DDC 798.83--dc23

Manufactured in the United States of America

# CONTENTS

# HOP ON THE SLED

Many people find the thrill of a lifetime falling through the air with a **parachute**, some climbing the tallest mountain in the world. But others, like the ones you'll learn about in this book, prefer traveling fast through the icy cold with a big pack of dogs. They love a sport called sled dog racing!

Imagine crossing the frozen Arctic on the back of a dogsled. You stand on the **runners** as your team tries not to slip on the ice-covered ground. All around you, the icy wind and snow whip across your face. People use sled dogs for transportation, to have fun, or to race against others. The most famous sled dog race in the world is called the Iditarod.

# A LIFESAVING SLED DOG RACE

In 1925, a great blizzard struck in Alaska during an epidemic. Only a team of **mushers** could carry medicine to Nome, Alaska, saving many lives. The modern Iditarod race has remembered this historic event by naming an honorary musher in memory of Leonhard Seppala. Seppala is a musher who raced 264 miles (425 km) with a sled dog team to help deliver the lifesaving medicine to Nome.

ALASKANS USED SLED DOGS TO TRANSPORT GOODS, MEDICINE, AND MAIL BEFORE PLANES AND CARS CAME INTO WIDE USE.

# CHALLENGES OF THE RACE

Finishing any sled dog race is a challenge. Many who attempt the about 1,000 mile (1,609 km) Iditarod race between Anchorage and Nome, Alaska, fail. They, or their dogs, become ill from little sleep and lack of food. And spending more than a week—sometimes as many as three weeks—mostly alone in the wilderness takes a mental **toll**.

So, why race the Iditarod? Some people love the danger of the trail! Others honor the tradition of sled dogs bringing mail to gold mining camps in the early 1900s. But, of course, there's also the glory—and about $500,000 of prize money—waiting for the finishers! In the 2023 race, Ryan Redington won $51,800 for coming in first place.

## MAN'S BEST FRIEND

Joe Redington Sr., known as the Father of the Iditarod (and Ryan Redington's grandfather), said he likes dogsledding because, "I've seen **snow machines** break down and fellows freeze to death out there in the wilderness. But dogs will always keep you warm and they'll always get you there."

EVEN THOUGH HIS GRANDFATHER WAS ONE OF THE FOUNDERS OF THE IDITAROD, RYAN REDINGTON WAS THE FIRST PERSON IN HIS FAMILY TO WIN THE RACE.

# RULES OF THE RACE

To compete in the Iditarod today, there are many rules teams must follow. The rulebook states: "The race should be won or lost by the musher and dogs on merit rather than on **technicalities**." That means a team should win because of its abilities and not because of a minor rule. Therefore, training is very important!

Mushers must be 18 years old and use a team of 12 to 14 dogs. At least five dogs must still be attached to the sled at the end of the race. To race in the Iditarod, a musher must have finished an earlier race—the Yukon Quest International Sled Dog Race, or two 300-mile (483 km) qualifying races plus one other qualifying race to equal 750 miles (1,207 km).

# HOW FAR?

The official length of the Iditarod race is 1,049 miles (1,688 km), a reference to the fact that Alaska is the 49th state in the United States. Technically, though, the land mushers and dog sleds cover is a little less than 1,000 miles (1,609 km).

DURING EVEN YEARS, THE IDITAROD USES A NORTHERN PART OF THE IDITAROD NATIONAL HISTORIC TRAIL. IN ODD YEARS, MUSHERS TRAVEL A SOUTHERN SECTION.

# TIME TO TRAIN

Training for long-distance sled dog races is necessary not only to win a race but also to keep the dogs safe. Sled dogs may start training as puppies. Early on, they learn commands such as come, sit, and stay. They are also given chances to explore their natural surroundings. At around 6 months old, the puppies can wear a harness for the first time. Then, the dogs begin learning about pulling a sled and racing!

Mushers choose their smartest and speediest dogs to be at the front of the team. These "lead dogs" have a very close connection with their musher. Experienced lead dogs are often paired with those in training to show them how to act on the trail. For example, dogs in training must be able to quickly untangle themselves from the **gangline**.

# ALASKAN HUSKY

The best dogs for sled racing are a mixed breed called the Alaskan husky. These dogs are smart and easy to train. They're bred especially for speed, endurance, attitude, and ability to handle extreme weather conditions.

BEFORE THEY CAN BE ATTACHED TO THE GANGLINE WITH THE MORE EXPERIENCED DOGS, MUSHERS HAVE PUPPIES RUN ALONGSIDE THE SLED TO LEARN THE ROPES.

Hot or cold, snow or not, mushers train their sled dogs all year long. Because of their extra-thick coats, though, sled dogs can easily overheat during the summer. But they still need to train, so mushers take the dogs on routes or paths with lots of puddles or bodies of water so they can cool off. By the fall, more structured training can start.

What about the mushers themselves? They must be very fit and have a lot of mental focus. But training with the dogs, especially when winter comes and the dogs can pull sleds on the snow, is the best way for mushers to prepare for the Iditarod. The dogs learn to trust and listen to their musher, who relies on certain spoken commands to lead the team.

MUSHERS TRAIN THEIR DOGS WITH TREATS AND WORDS OF PRAISE.

# LISTENING TO COMMANDS

Mushers direct their dogs through spoken commands. Here are some of the most common terms heard on the trail.

| MUSHING COMMAND | MEANING |
|---|---|
| GEE | turn right |
| HAW | turn left |
| LINE OUT | a command to tell the lead dog to pull the team straight out from the sled |
| WHOA | stop |
| HIKE, ALL RIGHT, LET'S GO | start |

# CHOOSING A SLED

Mushers have some options when it comes to selecting a sled for racing. There are two main types of sleds—basket sleds and toboggan sleds. Basket sleds have a flatbed that is raised above the runners, allowing mushers to store gear underneath. Toboggan sleds are directly connected to the runners.

The rules state that each musher can choose any type of sled but that it "must be capable of hauling any injured or fatigued dogs under cover, plus equipment and food." Mushers are allowed to use up to three different sleds during the race.

The sleds aren't much different from those used in the past. Sleds were originally made only of wood, but now they use different materials, including steel, plastic, **titanium**, **aluminum**, **carbon fiber**, and wood.

## SUITING UP!

All the dogs on a sled team have collars and harnesses connecting them to the ropes they use to pull the sled. There are different harness styles for different breeds or body types of dogs. Some harnesses are better for lean dogs, while others work better for stouter dogs.

THIS MUSHER USES A BASKET SLED—WITH THE RAISED FLATBED—WHILE HER DOGS ARE ATTACHED WITH WHAT'S CALLED AN X-BACK HARNESS, THE MOST COMMON TYPE OF HARNESS IN SLED DOG RACING.

# LOADING UP THE GEAR

What mushers carry on their sled is just as important as the sled itself. Iditarod racers must carry certain items, including a notebook used by the veterinarians who take care of the dogs along the trail. These are called "vet books." Each musher also packs a cold weather sleeping bag, an axe, and snowshoes, as well as a set of eight booties for each dog to protect their feet.

Mushers also bring extra pairs of insoles to go inside their boots and socks, eye goggles or sunglasses, ski poles, and a knife. Additionally, they pack trail mail, which is symbolic of the historic use of sled dogs to deliver mail. Other items mushers pack include fuel, a cooking pot, enough food for the dogs and themselves, and a backup emergency supply of food.

## SPECIAL FOOTWEAR

Sled dogs have special footwear! They wear booties to protect from **frostbite**. They also protect the dogs' feet from ice balls forming between their toes, sharp objects on the trail, and the heavy toll running can take on paws.

SLED DOGS ARE TRAINED TO LIFT THEIR PAWS TO HELP MUSHERS PUT THE BOOTIES ON THEIR FEET.

# WEATHER ON THE TRAIL

Once on the trail, mushers are completely in charge of their dog team and all the decision making. While mushers can control their pace, one trail condition they can't control is the weather. Typically, temperatures stick around freezing, or 32°F (0°C) along the route.

Temperatures can fall to -40°F (-16°C), made worse by dangerous, or unsafe, howling winds and blowing snow. The race route is known for terrible snowstorms that can stop sled teams wherever they are!

If the temperatures inch up above freezing—still cold for humans—it could be too warm for the dogs! Sled dogs are bred to have extra thick coats, so they race best in temperatures from -20°F (-29°C) to 20°F (-7°C). With any higher temperature, they run the risk of overheating as they run.

## CLIMATE CHANGE

In recent years, climate change has made running the Iditarod more difficult. Increasing temperatures mean less snow will be on the ground. The snow that is there is slushy and hard to race on. Race organizers have had to change or shorten the route during extra warm years.

IN 2016, THERE WAS SO LITTLE SNOW ON THE GROUND IN ANCHORAGE, IDITAROD ORGANIZERS HAD TO BRING IN SNOW FROM FAIRBANKS FOR THE CEREMONIAL START OF THE RACE!

# CHECKING IN

Checkpoints are an important part of the Iditarod race. They can vary from a simple cabin in the woods to more elaborate camping sites where teams can resupply. According to the race rules, teams in the Iditarod must take a full 24-hour stop at a place and time of their choosing. They must also take two 8-hour stops at certain points.

Checkpoint stops are very important for both the dogs' and musher's safety and health. Veterinarians look over the dogs and give any needed medical attention. If a dog is too sick to continue, it's left behind at these points to be cared for. Mushers and dogs eat and drink lots of water at checkpoints. Depending on the route, there are about two dozen checkpoints.

# FUELING UP

During checkpoints, sled dogs eat a lot! Mushers must be prepared with about 2,000 pounds (908 kg) of meat, dry dog food, and even fish and vitamins for their team during the Iditarod. More importantly, each musher carries a cooker and fuel to use it. The cooker melts snow to make water for the dogs to drink.

THE FINGER LAKE CHECKPOINT IS NEAR WINTERLAKE LODGE, WHERE THE OWNERS ARE KNOWN FOR COOKING UP MEALS FOR THE MUSHERS.

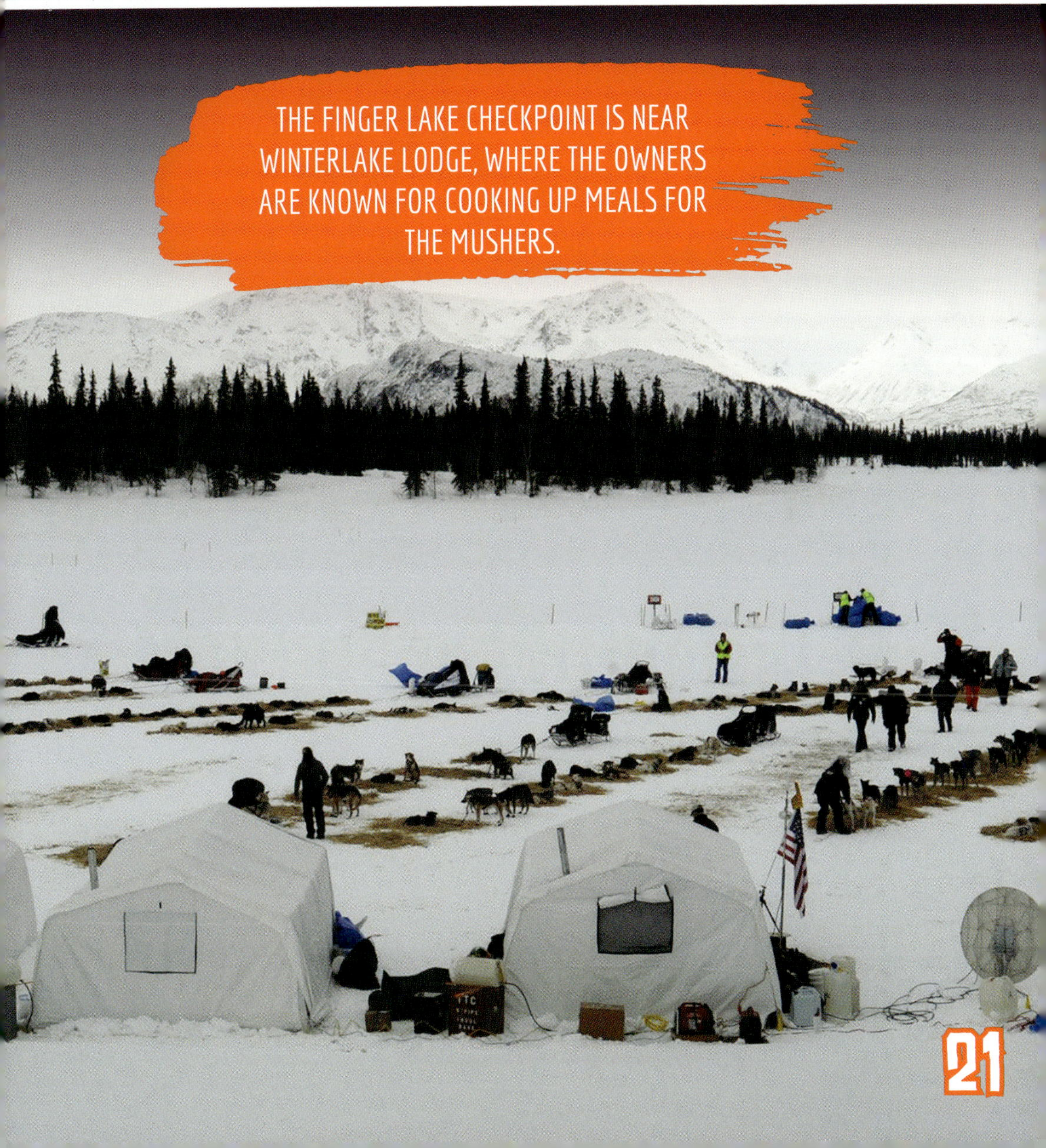

# DANGER IN THE SNOW

Legendary Iditarod musher Susan Butcher fell through thin ice several times throughout her career. Most notably, nearly her entire team fell through ice in 1984 during the Iditarod. Though her lead dogs were able to pull her out, Butcher's experience shows how unpredictable—and dangerous—racing the Iditarod can be. For many, the riskiness itself is exciting. Still, a huge moose threatening a dog team would probably cause even the most daring musher to be nervous.

Mushers pay a physical price during the race. Their hands become covered in blisters. Their wet, cold feet can freeze. If they don't sleep enough, they may start seeing things. Sometimes these dangers occur miles away from anyone who can help!

## IDITAROD AIR FORCE

Iditarod daredevils aren't just on the trail—they're above it. The Iditarod Air Force, made up of about two dozen volunteers, helps supplies and volunteers get from place to place along the long race route. However, it's a dangerous job. The weather is often rough for flying.

SUSAN BUTCHER, PICTURED SLEDDING ACROSS THE BERING SEA ICE IN 1992, WAS THE SECOND WOMAN TO WIN THE IDITAROD. SHE WON THREE YEARS IN A ROW—FROM 1986 TO 1988. SHE ALSO WON IN 1990.

Sled dogs experience danger both during the race and during preparations. Some become **dehydrated** and overheated. Dogs can cut their paws, and sometimes they get sick. For mushers, dogs' injuries or illnesses are part of the risk they take by competing in the race. But sometimes, dogs die.

In 2013, a 5-year-old dog named Dorado died after he was covered with snow overnight and couldn't breathe. His death was an accident, as sled dogs commonly sleep in snow to keep warm. However, Dorado wasn't the first Iditarod death. In 2009, six dogs died, five died in 2017, and one died in 2019. Many dogs are also injured or killed during breeding, training, and from long-term problems after the race.

## WORTH THE DANGER?

The Iditarod is tough, some say too tough on the dogs. People for the Ethical Treatment of Animals (PETA), a group that works for animal rights, is against the Iditarod. Though there's a rule stating that the dogs should be treated well, PETA reports that more than 150 Iditarod sled dogs died between 1973 and 2023.

A VETERINARIAN WHO VOLUNTEERED WITH THE IDITAROD SAID THE MOST COMMON PROBLEMS HE SAW WITH DOGS WERE FROSTBITE, SHOULDER INJURIES, AND **DIARRHEA**.

# CROSSING THE FINISH LINE

Around 100 people and their dog teams usually race in the Iditarod each March, and some have had memorable finishes! In 1978, Dick Mackey and Rick Swenson raced into Nome right next to each other. Both no longer stood on their sleds' runners and were running next to their teams. When they crossed the finish line on Front Street, no one knew who won. An Iditarod official ruled that the nose of the lead dog from Mackey's team crossed the finish line first! It was the closest finish in the Iditarod's history.

Dick Mackey's racing skills run in the family. His son Rick won the race in 1983. His other son, Lance Mackey, holds the current record for the most **consecutive** Iditarod wins at four! In 2019, Pete Kaiser became the first Yup'ik—and fifth Alaskan Native—to win the race.

## A RACE FOR THE KIDS

Thrill seekers come in all ages. In fact, mushers ages 14 to 17 can race in the 150-mile (241 km) Junior Iditarod! In 2005, Dallas Seavey became the first person to race the Junior Iditarod and the Iditarod in the same year. In 2023, Emily Robinson became the first young woman to win the race twice!

PETE KAISER, WHO WON THE IDITAROD IN 2019, POSES WITH HIS LEAD DOGS.

Sled dogs have also earned their fair share of attention. In 2022, a dog named Leon ran off from his team at a checkpoint. His owner, musher Sébastien Dos Santos Borges, said Leon slipped out of his collar and coat. Leon was missing for nearly three months before locals in McGrath, Alaska, reported seeing him. He was found nearly 150 miles (241 km) away from where he went missing at the Ruby checkpoint!

Locals fed Leon and were eventually able to catch him. Iditarod organizers said the dog was skinny but seemed healthy when he was found. Leon was reunited with Dos Santos Borges a few days later, and the pair were able to return to their home country of France.

## THE YUKON QUEST SPLIT

The 1,000-mile (1,600 km) race between Whitehorse in Yukon Territory, Canada, and Fairbanks, Alaska, was once known as an even tougher race than the Iditarod. The Yukon Quest split up into two races in 2022, though. There's now one race in Canada and one in Alaska.

THE IDITAROD SHOWS THE IMPORTANCE OF STAYING HEALTHY PHYSICALLY AND MENTALLY IN EXTREME SITUATIONS!

# GLOSSARY

**aluminum:** A silver metal that's both strong and light.

**carbon fiber:** A strong, lightweight material made of carbon.

**consecutive:** Following one after the other in a certain order.

**dehydrated:** Having lost a lot of water from the body.

**diarrhea:** A sickness in which a person or animal passes waste quickly and in a liquid form from their body.

**frostbite:** A condition in which part of the body freezes.

**gangline:** The lines or ropes that connect the sled dogs together to the sled.

**musher:** The human who rides on and directs a dogsled.

**parachute:** A piece of equipment often made of cloth and used to slow a person who is falling through the air.

**runners:** The two bottom pieces of a dogsled that touch the snow.

**snow machine:** Another name for a snowmobile, a vehicle made for traveling through the snow.

**technicality:** A small detail in the rules of a competition.

**titanium:** A strong, light, silvery metal.

**toll:** A serious or bad effect on a person or animal.

# FOR MORE INFORMATION

## BOOKS

Berne, Emma Carlson. *Balto*. New York, NY: Scholastic Press, 2022.

Klepeis, Alicia. *Sled Racing Dogs*. Minneapolis, MN: SportsZone, 2019.

Shulman, Mark, and Solomon Shulman. *Siberian Huskies*. Minneapolis, MN: Bigfoot Books, 2021.

## WEBSITES

**History Stories**
*www.history.com/news/the-sled-dog-relay-that-inspired-the-iditarod*
Read more about the 1925 event that inspired aspects of the Iditarod race.

**Iditarod**
*kids.britannica.com/kids/article/Iditarod/390068*
Learn more about the Iditarod race and the types of dogs that run in the sport.

**Iditarod: The Last Great Race**
*www.iditarod.com*
Visit the Iditarod's official website, which includes results, photos, and more history about the race.

# INDEX